Cross-Talk

To the loves of my life:
Kevin, Amy, Luke and Eoin

Siobhán Campbell
Cross-Talk

seren

Seren is the book imprint of
Poetry Wales Press Ltd.
57 Nolton Street, Bridgend, Wales, CF31 3AE
www.seren-books.com

The right of Siobhán Campbell to be identified as
the author of this work has been asserted in accordance
with the Copyright, Designs and Patents Act, 1988.

ISBN 978-1-85411-509-6

A CIP record for this title is available from the British Library.

The publisher acknowledges the financial assistance of the Welsh Books Council.

Cover Art: 'Untitled' woodblock on paper, 1990, by Mary Farl Powers, courtesy of
AIB Art Collection and the siblings of Mary Farl Powers.

Printed in Bembo by Bell & Bain, Glasgow.

Mixed Sources
Product group from well-managed
forests and other controlled sources
www.fsc.org Cert no. TT-COC-002769
© 1996 Forest Stewardship Council

FSC

Contents

I

II

III

"summoning pity...
by grief of kin...
till the whole tarnished map is stained and torn
not to be read as pastoral again"
                    – John Hewitt

"all poems... in varying degrees contain an internal conflict,
    cross-talk, back-wash, come-back or pay-off."
                    – Louis MacNeice

I

When all this is over

I plan to go north
by unapproved roads
where sniper signs rust on the trees.

I will cross the border
over and back
several times to see how it feels.

I will dance the pig's dyke
and taste mountain mayflower
on the breeze.

Near under-fished lakes
I will hear a blood-pause
in the reach of the night

when every word used for batter
and crisis will cruise with the ease
of what runs right through us,

when the shift and fill
of my own dear cells
is all they will tell as they breathe.

And out through the lanes,
I will lie in my form
in overgrown fields

not a chopper in sight.
And they say it is safe
and the weather agrees.

The last long drag

Evening, and smoke wells round the green flowers
on our walls. My father cannot quit although he knows
that aneurism loves his hard aorta, settles there
keeping its round plan. *Sweet~Afton*. If you breathe
in deep, the yellow box with big romantic letters gives
off a smell of stubbled meadow. Once he tried a silver
holder, longer and thinner than a finger, said it made
him feel a fop, or English. He took to tipped but broke
their filters off. Otherwise they may as well be air.
He doesn't need the exercise. He must be lit before
he'll take the phone and flicks one-handed, as he goes
to get the door. Between car and church there's a few
last porch-dark pulls, then out with a stamp and in to god.
Mornings we can hear him cough to shift the phlegm
that lines his chest. He hacks to break its grip and spits.
Then there's the lighting of the first. When he talks
of the north, of girls tarred and feathered for loving
from the wrong camp, he calls them wretches. This night,
tied to a lamp post there was one in tatters. Tar streaked
her freckles. They had given her a Sweet Afton.
It sounded as though nothing worse could happen.

The ripening of an R.U.C. man

First it was Spanish guitar, she paid for the lessons;
thought it a sign he was coming back to himself.
He wanted a chord that smelled of ripening oranges,
felt he could spy the secret door of the Alhambra.
There were amps and clamps, all kinds of gadgets
but they don't hold the balls like a bull does.
After a week, it was cycling. Seven hundred quid
on a top of the range. He could be a *Tour* impostor
but those gears must not be right for hills.
He had to get off and walk it up. There's a shed full
of wheels, gathering dust. He took up pot-bellied pigs.
Two. They like company. They're locked in the lounge.
He handles the moss they eat as if it is pieces of scorched
flesh gathered from roofs; sent back with a plastic
bag to follow the crows. So she wasn't surprised
when he went out on the small lake, a marl hole really,
took the row boat with its two oars, one jiggery,
pulled himself to the dead centre past the reeds,
felt the sway of the boat and stood, straddled.
Did he call them in? How do you call fish your prey?
Well they came, surrounded him with their butt heads
and slick-flip tails, lapping, circling. He took the rifle,
heavy shouldered, loaded up, leaned full-sighted
and shot the pike, one by one, each in its writhing head.

Campbell

"I shall never deny those who came to this gnarled coast
with a skinful of sopped hope and started with their brood
this trail that would become the family you call yours.

You know in Ulster Scots they don't use the word 'lane'
but have to say 'wee road'. The laming of a tongue
will map it out of mind unless it has a name.

Raymond, Ursula, the two Hughs, who laid on betting sheets,
knew when to settle odds and how to be discreet,
paid blind to the sidelong flutter of small groups.

They each made one more shift from anything that marked,
though wondered through two wars what way to stream a lay
for those come home in droves from fights that were not ours.

I am the last.

Though you are from the south, you need to find the will
to hold a vowel too long. Tell people by their heed
and know who must be paid. Keep always your own name.
It takes a softened tongue to fill a twisted mouth."

Creed

By the tap of his shoes, we know him,
by the shunt of his vowels. We groomed him
from birth to be ours. Even on days in the mountains,
he's behind us in the lull of the trees.

Tap, tap he goes, striking fear into the follicles
of young girls. Their hair shaved off, their bodies
brushed and we knew if he could,
he would cut out their tongues.

To feel his power, I was brought on a march,
to the sound of horns, a colour party, their buttons
sparkle, the gleam of the guns. Are they for us?
Are they for us really?

With a wisp of whine, we sang them a ballad
of our lost youth. They closed us down. No time
to learn a hymn re-laid by hands shot through
in the hold of prayer. It's a new divine.

They can think all things at once. We're dizzy
with spin. The store I shop in, they own.
The van that delivers is freshly sprayed.
What is their game?

Their mandate is precious, they press the mandators.
They are not insane. That shriek you hear is
an ear too close to the source. Soon they will enter
the imagination where they wait to put it out.

Will of the People

If, in the many-spangled cheek of a high wire walker,
the print of a footstep edges toward her pretty ear;
if she is used by the elephant act before the interval
while out back the hippo is hosed down to keep him cool
and in the tent this lumbering creaser is approaching
her small white cheek and the fool signals the foot to fall —
Elephant keeper, how could you let it happen?
How could you take us to the brink of ourselves,
knowing that we make her fly through our sparked clapping,
how we swing our emotional track when she runs the wire?
We could nearly have cried if the moment became a story.
Given all this, that it is ruined, will we return, chanting slogans
about cruelty, root you off that green we laid near the parks?

Quickthorn

Don't bring haw into the house at night
or in any month with a red fruit in season
or when starlings bank against the light,
don't bring haw in. Don't give me reason
to think you have hidden haw about you.
Tucked in secret, may its thorn thwart you.
Plucked in blossom, powdered by your thumb,
I will smell it for the hum of haw is long,
its hold is low and lilting. If you bring
haw in, I will know you want me gone
to the fairies and their jilting. I will know
you want me buried in the deep green field
where god knows what is rotting.

Pitched

Here, in our own time, a living memory
exists of a man who made nature out of mind.
A bent man, curved in a crook, who skewed
the ash trees, tied them down, flexed them
until the arc of his wishing came to be
and they reached toward their full becoming.
These were the unimaginable hayforks, all
of a piece, no maker's mark, a tine so precise
it made lifting two bales entirely possible.
Yes, they were for sale but at a price,
a different amount for every purchaser, a sum
to be reckoned after a month, their time
to coddle the sweep of the instrument in
newly worn hands, when they felt it sway
in the dip of one finger, and could watch
the wood seize their thumb print, its first knots
smoothed out of nodules. Put aside, laid down
and walked away from in a barn, or propped
in a rack, a branch might begin in a dint of work.
And were it forgotten, left like a body in the dark
it might slip out a root. But this is conjecture.
What is certain is that these hayforks
would never warp, once bent.

Removal

This morning
  a hare stood stem–still
    watching my door open square

Sodden look of thud and tear
  hock sworn speed
    the zip of fields into halves

What motioned him to start
  race from a dented den
    where grass unfolds his form?

His breath more white
  more of it on the air than mine
    from a smaller heart

I see the brown eye
  of the spied replicator
    is counting me out

Beyond my lintel
  home recedes
    until it is vastly gone

His seize on the day
  thickens time
    like a bomb

Blind Eye

Beware the man who ploughed a fairy ring.
He wouldn't be stopped by tale or deed
though moss fell off his roof in clumps
and starlings abandoned his haggart.

He hoped the cypress would not see,
by the strobe light high on his tractor,
how the whites of his eyes had already pooled
with things you can tell no neighbour.

He kept china dogs on his mantle,
one had a painted monocle;
Three monkeys down by the hearth
gathered to say no evil.

He never thought of the roots of trees
stalled in their reaching mirror,
the desperate effort of their shift
as diesel fumes came nearer.

Beware the man who forgets,
who sees his wheat ripen like gangrene,
the best of it splayed in a patch of flat
that others swear is a ring.

That other walking stick

Her father too had an ash-black stick
he used to whack the heads off weeds.
He thwacked off the foxglove heads
with the stick he acquired when he was lamed.

He sent them flying, pinks and reds,
with a swish and flick of his black walking stick.
The pinks and reds flew through the air
like bullets sure-fired and purposely there.

The flowers broke apart the air
like gullets of blood smattering there.
With a swish and rick of the black ash stick
her father left the lane bare of heads

and the stalks remained alive though maimed
without their beauty pinks and reds.
Without their beauty pinks and reds
they lived on though seemed to be dead

while petals were scattered and smattered there
where the ashen stick laid everything bare.

Hothead

He could name all these, wildflowers of the Mournes
and because there was a story to be told, he could pull
through breast and brains the way they took these names
from a distant past, a past before there rose a single god
under whom the outrage was to wage.

He would name them and the stamen of their being
stood still in the act of naming. The scent of them flew
out from his tongue, a balm to the legendary wounding.

And he would touch each petal, there, like that, between
a fat finger and a solid thumb, yet not bruise it,
but trace and lift it up as if that too would clear, would hold
the sound still in the valley and resound it out beyond,
yes, let it fly to its death in a sodden sky.

You are never just out, walking a field

If there's land for sale in the barony of Mourne,
you'll have the world and his mother up to take a look.
One will be after a stray sheep say, or a rogue dog
or they might be checking an ancient right of way.
Whatever excuse, they'll be there alone at dusk,
footing its width, counting the thistles with a stick.
They know how soil cools time down, how it holds
sweat and groan, worry for weather and the long wait.

What moan sounds to a keen ear from the seven
acre field? Seven sorry acres given to marry her,
dowried for five years until it was time to hand it back
though it still held the seed of last season, their first
good yield, and the timid beginnings of their marriage.
Come then you who have ears to hear him sob
as he beat her so her brothers would fear she'd be found
by the railway acre. Or you, who can tap the dull click
in her throat as she retches back to will him on –
for only a broken sister would convince her kin.

The Enthusiast

To the glorious, pious and immortal memory
Of the great and good who came to aid us,
Who so assisted in redeeming us from slavery
Arbitrary power, brass money and wooden shoes.

May we want before they want.

And all who drink this, whether he be priest, deacon,
Bellows-blower, grave digger or any other of the fraternity,
May a north wind blow him to the south
And a west wind to the east,
May he never have a dark night, a lee shore, a rank storm
Or a leaky vessel to carry him over the River Styx.

And as for the tap, the smote, the runt, the scamp,
Who thinks fire should be tamed with a poker,
May the dog Cerberus make a meal of his rump
And Pluto a snuff box of his skull,
And may the scald jump down his throat
And eat him out
And with every pin tear through his gut
And blow him, carcass clean, to the far ends of the earth.

North

The high shelves of your shop are full of pawn.
Behind the counter, bets are taken down.
That old tea tin with its Chinese scene, false
bottom for the chits in blue Cross pen,
a fount of code to stroke the family pulse
in case they ever need to take a turn.

Where a rimmed sufficiency is elegant,
enunciated quietly through restraint.
Swings tied up on a Sunday. Couldn't bear
the whoosh of coming back to earth?
Where art was naught and nil was a figure
tic-tacked through years of odds that finished worse.

How you pitched the salt in the soup.
I'm from the Dodge, only passing through.
The view down both forks off the Antrim Road.
And the Snipe who wished he had a big boil
heaped on his neck, to tease his hands, corrode
his nail until it burst. Pus like yellow oil.

What you smelt arriving in by boat. Doubt.
Fish guts on the wind. Pebble docked
to the click of skittering nerve.
You at the meeting place where no-one came.
You hadn't allowed for *lost.* A swerve
begins, longer than the trail of name.

Every question has to have an answer.
Think of nothing dark or true or tender
but watch us slide from absolute to bland.
Wait now till we see what way's the wind,
till we check the lie of the land.
We'll not put money on it, mind.

Small wonder we are best over soft ground,
settled for our own bit of bog.
What, after the huff and puff, is fiddled and fried?
For pawn, read porn. We cannot tell the decoy
from the damned, but manage an autonomy of guile.
Our genes are thick with doubt that makes us coy.

First Time Up

How could we catch their weird? They speak so fast.
We flip the ashtrays in a borrowed car, the driver worries
where to park and we're becoming cousinly through lives
slid from under a remark. What would they expect?
Not the blue-bruised roses that we brought them by the root.

They might be out on nights we're in our beds, setting snares
in the whin that we call furze. We thought we knew the island.
Theirs is colonised. Pine martens occupy the roof.
A hum of bees warms a hidden loft, the line of sparrows
stuffed to look alive. Someone must dust.

We see them reel with hands that stroke the coats
of ferrets sent down-warren. Hung in their bunks
we'll sway away the distance from that skiff, feeling
the edge of likely waters, the swelling that could drown us.
Suck of bait digging, nip of fly-tying in their riddled nails,
nest spots and the fiddle of egg swapping.

Two-headed lamb

You were nearly stuffed
for *Believe it or Not*.
You could have put Saul, County Down on the map.
But someone remembered
there was one with three heads
that lived for a day and a bit in Saskatchewan
and the taxidermist did such a job
you think all six eyes follow you round
the exhibit in Ripleys, Niagra Falls.
So we killed it quick
in Saul, County Down
where if we cannot cull you
nobody can.

Defined by negatives

Not now the fine thought, a spill of whistle notes
trilled to a pitch of the passionate past.
No more the tight ream
spun to a sum that will not balance.

Fierce indignation is best understood
by those who have no hope in its real good.
Whether a thought wound can be healed by thought
depends on how you treat the non-receiving heart.

One of our own will shed the sham most surely.
Behind the flummery, there's thlummery,
beyond the hokum, bunkum.

It takes blarney to sell boloney.
Those with a titter of wit are used.
The rest are twisted from a cast that never fit.

Hinterland

I move a step too close
and blow into his face
the match he lit to check
whether I have his wit.

The boy that he KO'd
made him an instant man
who rang the counting down
and turned toward the known.

A bout of wintering
along the outer rim
where Antrim makes intention
or else we learn to sing.

Tune of the clammed cold
of water under sand.
I tap it with my thumb
and hear the basalt slide.

One way to win the past
is not to frill between.
Next time I'll catch the flame
in my pre-heated palm.

Still Life

In the sunflower field, a multitude of will.
Each stalk reaches for a known god.
Every day a new dawn pulls life juice
from root tips to the first gathering petals.

They make themselves in the image of their lord.
Sun heads turning, sun heads rising
east to west as their ruler moves over
the sky he owns, over the earth he burns.

Loyal to the source, they watch for a sign
he sees, for any nod toward their longing.
A dread they tell in the dark of night
is of his not returning.

They have to be good. They must dream
sun dreams in their fitful sleep. They will
count the hours until they can wake, feel
their stretch as his first rays curl over the hill.

When this is the field of bent heads,
long on sun, lolled over tall stalks
still able to turn, they will dry up,
their seeds pressed out.

Tired, but not sad in their last days,
they will love the sun more
for not turning away
from their slow-necked deaths.

Crossing by Ferry

We try to heed the tiny signs
lodged behind his rheumy eyes,
how we are sized up for weight
as regulars file on in.
We had imagined tattooed arms
but couldn't stare to read.
The wallet at the back of his thigh
is packed with fares.
Is the woman in grey coming or going?
She coughs something up onto her chest
and leaves it there as an answer.

Out from shore the current knows
which waves to hitch and kick.
Does Skipper see how we
are trying to keep an even breath?
The lough fjord spits where summer's shift
is brimmed to seethe and slap.
His eyes have watered out of cloud.
We grip the slats.
Once parallel to the other pier,
he calls out – *Everyone off.*
But docking us is swayed and slow.
He watches as we scrape and pull
at odds with our arrival.

Pepper

Scallups was your word for sliced potato
fried in a medley of lard, scooped
from the corners of pans we kept
and cooled to save the solid sards,
flavoured with whatever had been cooked,
a week of smells in one Friday dinner.
At the shoreline you would skim pebbles;
flatties hipped and skished the water.
Scallops you would name the shells,
that long thin one, brown and doubled over
a white infill. Later I learned, a razor-shell.

Up at Clonallon graveyard you caught rabbit,
skinned them alive with a special knife.
They kicked to scald but you were fearless.
A pink whiteness would be tendered bright
in a pan where scaul becomes a rabbit paw,
its descender *die* still missing from the dinner.
We'd watch you fold in scallions with the mash
as if you made colcannon. I know, if they read
your DNA, it could take years to isolate the point
at which you learned to say the *a* in salt
the way it made a holy sea of spice.

Parsing

It was not the dresser, slant against the wall
where poltergeist had shattered every plate,
or the black cat no-one owned to own
that took up pole position for the scraps.
It wasn't just their gangers having names,
or that the field where everything seemed fair
was where a hand boomed up across a flower.

It may have been the settle edge of words
sucked against the bite of damson jam,
No Fraternising fisted on the walls
we took to be a reference to our nerve.
Or else it was the fright of being seen
by those who know a helicopter strobe
can seal the eye that watches from within.

Biography

Father: "We tried and tried and nothing happened
yet all the time we were waiting for you in the keen of night.
We had thermometers and she would tell me when not to go
to the pub with the lads. She didn't like keeping the dinner
warm over a pot of water. Her gravy would congeal
and I'd have to eat from the centre of the plate to the edge
in curling circles like a shell. So she was glad when the
temperature said it was time and we tried. Still nothing.
Your mother's mother died six days after she was born
and her mother before her in the throes of pain. Bad blood,
poison in the veins. She was afraid, though beyond her to say."

Mother: "He wouldn't go to bed with me, called me a sex
maniac if I asked him. After all, we were married and he
promised we could try for a family if I moved back to Ireland.
There we were in Dublin in a lovely little flat with a grand bed
and still he would avoid it. Thought I should have an Immaculate
Conception, until I wore him down because he knew what
side his bread was buttered on, that I was the winner of that bread,
and the pocket money he brought in wouldn't keep a fly in dung.
I only muttered the word *annulment* once but it was enough.
He came to bed that night and you were conceived, though
I didn't know if I was giving life to my death."

Daughter: "When I swam to the over-face, I knew there was
no going back. It is all documented: birth cert, photos,
the priest with the blue-blank eye. Scanned and scared,
I would have to approximate the movement of a *me*, grow
to fit the lock curled in an envelope. Perfect unlistening
became my primary nature. They would not tell the making
of a shape shifter. If beginning to trace the contour of a self,
I remembered the first question: Are we more than figment,
less than preservation? I hear their stories in the weave of my
waking, nothing more familiar or more strange."

II

These Women

"These men are no dreamers"
— MacDiarmid, 'The Wreck of the Swan'

These women are no dreamers.
They make happen the full wake,
the kettle hopping, the oven warm.

They take death in hand
and force him to be civil.
In their lighting, the spitting candle calms
and the rosary settles out of irony.

These women are not kind
if you do not iron the sheets you borrowed,
if you bring batch instead of sliced,
what good is that for sandwiches?

These women bar all holds in the
screamed stall of the birthroom.
Instead they ask for the gummed grit
they found for themselves in that
most alone of coupled moments.

These women know how to mash potatoes
so that they charge despair
out of a teenager.

They have followed a father
and a small child on a combine harvester,
not to pick up the pieces of the boy's arm

and bring them to his mother,
but because they felt the call of the back field
like something rotting in the feed shed
before chief rat jumps out.

These women will not pass through
the horse meadow, even on a summer night,
for there they have felt that the world might let us go.

They've seen the consequence of that.
Ironing keeps it at bay
and doing what is right.

Giving the Talk

I know every stick and stone of this old road
every hollyhock and foxglove
where the flesh fly lays her eggs in devil spit;
which hedges harbour the blackthorn
and where to pick the best berries, high up
and low down. Like us all, round here,
I know which corner the articulated lorry
jackknifed, taking a shortcut off the main road,
scattering the limbs of the two Brady children
on either side. No-one put flowers
or one of those little crosses. Slowing down
on that bend, as everyone here knows,
is treacherous.

Return

That he was taken out of the corn and beat,
I can believe. The big man who
runs the farm used a length of pipe –
whatever was to hand that would hurt
and he wasn't thinking of Ireland
when he did it either.
But why the young lad walked back
out of the yard the following week,
why he stood they say for hours
in the midst of the stalks, the ears;
their multitude, their sway quietening
his mind maybe.
Did he think something could happen
if he watched the growing of a living thing,
still enough so the mice ran around him
and a frog sat on the toe of his boot;
Did he think he could make up
for stoning Bat's puppies to a bloody mess
by the schoolyard wall?
If it was a circle itself he was planning to make
when the sun left,
well, you could nearly reason that;
but beat he was, to within a shred of his life.
Though the pelvis set
they say he'll walk with a limp
and no girl will have him
from here to the far side of Merton's cross.

Famished

In a hurl of rain
in a heedless fog
in winds that are indifferent
did you think of yourselves
out on the edge of Europe
as a trammelled people

or was the scored pill
of bread in the mouth enough;
comfort of tongued nights
the slant scald of climax –
and what you thought of
in counting the days to blight?

Sinister

it's not a right, it's a preference
to sit on the left side of the lord
swing down the sinistral and god I know it well
how to make ends meet, how to cut my cloth to suit my measure
wear the cuffs long so they might not see
the mark of the sinner
the troubles were never like this, *Citóg*
forced to write with your right
did you want to be saved or not
doing the work of the devil
and you could never hold a hurl right either
sure look at how you grip the knife
the way it would cut off more than you could chew
or blind the eye that is bigger than your stomach.

Platform

"My mother's yard was the cleanest one in Templeboy,"
the station master said as we waited for the ten eleven.
"In her haggart you could see the snips of granite glisten
like the promise of confetti shining up as you went by.
No rat ever darkened the door of her feed shed either
and as for the cattle, if they were in, she was after them
with a mop. She'd have yard-trained them if we'd let her.

There was one dip where a puddle settled, a filthy mirror.
She drove herself mad over how to be rid of that water.
How could she brush it away without making a muck?
She would nearly have sucked it up with the hoover
when she thought of the dog. The dog that needed
to drink or else be starved. So after rain, she brought
that mutt to water, finished off the job with lemon cleaner."

Now, you may think there was only him and me involved
in our encounter before the train arrived. But I could swear
I heard the muttering of another streel behind him as he ran
to wave his flag and that surely was the sound of something
parched that carped the distance just as I embarked.

Turns

Back and forth, over and back,
Don't you land on the concrete crack.
That's the line between here and never,
Skip on it and you won't go to heaven.

In and out, out and in,
How many times can you vote to win?
Fuss them down to town by train,
Then back home to vote again.

Over and back, up and over,
How many leaves in a four leafed clover?
One   two   three   four,
No you're wrong, it has one more,
The secret drill curled in the stem
That leaves the clover furl its whim.

Over and back, take up my slack,
One of us has to go to the back.
Gently mind or it skims a whip,
Watch the line, jump or trip.
Hold it straight or lose the tack.
Ah, you've slipped the concrete crack.

The run is broke.
The turn is took.
The rope is down.
And here's the dark.

Mercy

Nostalgia dies here at the point
where in-blown wrack is divvied out
and farmers hook their wariness
to friends that lately helped pull flax
or came at night to save a calf.

We're all down at the beach
whether our roof is slate or thatch.
Later, we'll meet to watch the smacks
willing them to wreck.
We're there already with our carts.

★★★

From Cranfield Point we watch,
willing the smacks to dock.
We're ready with our carts
whether our roof is slate or thatch.

We gather up the in-blown wrack
though some still hook their wary eyes
to friends that lately saved a calf
or bent their will in pulling flax.

Mother Ireland

We can tell by the weight of her step for how long she will shout.
When she roars there are words not words but shudders of hate.
They are riddled and ribbed into sounds not rendered but spat.
Or perhaps they are words in a world of sheet sore –
where no-one is born to ignore the value of work,
where no-one still lives who thinks money grows on trees,
where everyone knows to use their head for more than a hat.
They would not drive her out of her chinese mind.
They would not send her to the mental tearing her hair out.
They would have known the roast was to be kept for Sunday.
How could we have eaten our way through the freezer she packed
with a whole side of bullock? We must be big, in our own minds.
We should be re-sized in real life. This is why she will shout.
Now for as long as we live, she is making us fat.

How to get over trauma

Inevitably, you will have feelings you want to shed.
Here we need no bonfires, no bin lid cacophony
but a journey to find original purpose, embedded
deep beyond the tribal jag. There, you will be rid
of disinclination, see it for an inherited entropy.
We'll try to develop a sense of present attention.
But first, you must believe that you are loved.
The life peel of re-birthing is required. If tempted,
in the backtrack of the chamber, you may replay
the bloodfill of your story. Beware, an emptied
mind can make the darkening seasons gather.
Don't ask if spring will lengthen down your fingers,
the knuckles that have eased what felt like triggers.

Troubled

My father's foil,
A cousin once removed, signed up
For the Royal Irish Guards
Played rugby and deck quoits
On board a ship he built for
Workman Clark,
Drank gin with a twist
Voted for the Communists
Asked who carried on when Cain finished Abel,
Had it all to lose
Never wrote a word.

Or was he that other?
The one who turned
Fell for an Antrim princess
Pulled off a piece of causeway to keep,
Brought bad luck with it to the wains,
Smuggled petrol over the border
Cut growth hormone with talcum powder
Had three bulls in different fields
Developed a rare mini-marrow.

Idyll

Nothing was as it seemed to be lived.
We gave the nod to the big island every time,
went back there for work
and to find a land horizon.

We read death notices
sent solo in airmail envelopes
but couldn't remember
who was in school with whom.

Going along with it,
we were glad to be noticed.
Our forebears turned in their graves
until their fiction burned.

The sublime was a rocket of illusion
we sold to the other side,
then bought back again
coated with dye.

We saw them once through a doorway
gathered around a canoe
learning to bend fibreglass.
If we thought they would recognise us,
we were wrong.

When I asked my Dad about Warrenpoint

he said it was where folks gave up
grouse shooting and pheasant hunting for Lent,
where boys tongued it home with blackened mouths
after sucking the leaves of the aniseed bush
in the church grounds,
where once, at the dock dance, his sister
made him get back on the ferry without looking round
in case he would see his dead ringer.

She had given him, but not him, a jitterbug earlier,
her fright at the southern accent you could cut
and the look in his gamey eye.
She told Dad that he was the better looking, and she lied.
Still, it was best for the girls of two nations
that neither of them died.

Almost in sight

That was the summer of the early bees,
    of the big heat,
steam in the tamed street. We'd go up north,
It's always cooler by a few degrees,
take off, leave a smell of diesel on the tar,
glad that we would suck our stomachs in
at customs, braced for the questions,
Where are you going, where have you been?
spotting those braves, helmets branched in green,
out on manoeuvres on their knees.

All morning, we fight over the window,
    practice I spy,
put piggy in the middle
until the Cavan watchtower with one eye
comes into view, its high-up door benign.
It ducks, begins a peek-a-boo,
tucks in tight behind the hill. We pace
the road that's blasted through the drumlin,
knowing our tower is shifting side,
will pop right up as soon as we say *zero*.

We're told that summer inches over ground.
    No bees here yet,
but midges that gather in the dusk.
Trees slow to leaf have not quite hid
the sign, 'sniper at work'. Light fades
just as we'll leave, afraid our southern car
could lead to something more
than cousins spending time as planned.
Even the bread is different, comes in rounds,
farls quartered with a steady hand.

Away on roads so good it could be Mars,
    we'll look for change,
white street signs and painted kerbs,
places where they trade in fair exchange,
gluts of kids who stand around on bikes
with haircuts we have seen in magazines.
We'll stop to get some sweets we haven't tried,
new bars to keep for after lunch at Grans,
when we have lost the maze in willow plates
and go to visit graves with names like ours.

But look, we missed the cross; meant for the lark
    to ask the guard,
how many feet, how many inches from the posts,
if there's a line that lets you know your place,
and if they ever feel like slipping out and jumping
through at night, to say *I was in Ireland once.*
No matter, there's always next month's trip,
the day that Granny gets her pensions in,
she hands us pounds, clean and strange and crisp,
we grin at her majesty, check the watermark.

Bedding

The sow's in farrow
We need straw now
As much as you can carry
You have to hurry

We expect nothing though the night is bullioned
with stars that multiply between torch and
tar macadam. The joints of hawthorn hedge
are out for us and bramble branches that could
stripe an eye, but we dip and duck, streel
over the road in a flying column, unafraid
of gargoyles tusked in the trunks of crab apple.

Not built with brawn like our hardy cousins,
damp in their drained bones; barbed wire
may score us on the rigged stile but we'll prevail,
hauled to night-running from beds that hold winter
to the visitor, we'll run in a dream of sinew,
in a dream of farm, past spirit and charm, on up
the boreen to the neighbour's loomed barn.

No one said there would be loft and ladder,
a rickety fearful step-toe to the top; stacks
hid from thieves like us, packed into bales
wound with the devil's twine. We attack.
Pinches, then wrenches and wristed holes.
String-burned, stem-pocked hands. Mice scatter.
Rustle of straw cackles. The joke's on us.

Then down, down to the scooped mounds,
meshed armfuls, stuffed sweaters. A breath
of field in a sneeze pulled from the baler, force
pitted against his neat labour. We run with the fleet
of those born to save the day, to win against odds,
to keep as many bonamhs alive as would pay
for Christmas, glaze two hams at Easter.

What did it mean, the huff and puff, our
tightening steps, straw stranding from arms
that try to hold it in against a racked chest?
Running as if all depended, running for what
seemed our lives; back to the shed to spread
our loot for the pink-blind wriggling harvest.
Is that all you could manage?

Sow slow-lowering side rows of nipples
under and over the tufting hairs (for bristles,
for brushes?). Suckling them all, their snouted
globbering unstoppable. Except –
there is one too many. One who can't latch.
Kicked back, squeezed out, tries climbing.
The runt of the litter. He'll be dead by morning.

Lapping

What is it to lap hay in a western field,
shore side patched to the Atlantic?
Salt spray on the wind, a brace of thrusts
but calm in between, and a gladness
to be turning these bright rivers, stripes
of white gold, the life of winter feed.

What can it mean to lean and flip,
flip and lean, turn the fork in your wrist
and feel it prong? No blister today.
A frog jumps, still whole. Not the chopped
legs, green smears in hay. Currents are runnels
of fodder to turn and dry. We hope for sun.

Omeath to the Point

1947

Back then, it wasn't sheep rustling
diesel washing or money laundering

but strapping the pound of butter
to a cool thigh, taking the long walk

between two customs men
with nylons down our sleeves

and afterwards, the sin of pride
the same lordy lording.

2007

This is a crossing where waves can whip
a lough into a question. Though it is short,
one sea mile from south to north.

On the journey, notions of nation are suspended.
What a laugh we have at our customary selves.

When we arrive in the channel where only boats
of shallow draught may dare, we come to narrow water
and steady each other onto the swaying pier.

The Surprise

A landlady as mean as Ireland in the fifties.
The one boiled egg, "it's a cooked breakfast, isn't it?",
Towels with a rough touch exfoliate our skin;
A cowed son who looks as though she's worn him thin.
They despise us for staying at their meagre B and B.
She'll turn off the heat once we leave for the day.

In the breakfast room, above the no-brand cornflakes,
the red bloom of the Sacred Heart is bleeding.
And opposite, all smiles, an airbrushed JFK.
Two gods in one? They could do with a good cleaning.

She hears my thought. "I must take them down", she says,
"put Paisley there, Bigfoot though he is, he led,
and that other fellah, came back to the people in the end
and handsome enough I suppose, in his own way."

Grist

What is a mill? Six stark
floors, the smell of grain here still
and the stones in solid pairs
will not be parted, though someone
has tabbed names along their sides.
When did they last move?
Four couples, petrified; the way
they load against each other, life on life.

Beetling done, hammered out the strands,
the thread and its finish gone;
something else to keep the mill race
run; think of diameter,
a larger wheel, a greater breadth
of bucket, what it might mean
to spin beyond that range
hummed in the finetune of machine.

Tuck down, prepare to winnow out,
one pair of thickening frize
apiece and no new gadgets, just an
arm rest on which to show your metal.
Know there's always someone to pick
up the yarn, though they're getting younger,
ghosts that undershot the past
coming to breast into the future.

Stood in the kilnsman's house, the kiln
in sight, charred with a charmed heat.
Hear the wheel clap, the cry of *Up
Down* or *I'll send a bleacher to Tullylish.*
Every hand-scutch and I can feel inside
the point of those knitting needles
as she, employed there for that purpose,
eeks dirt from in between the tiles.

Weeding Mangels

The weeds we clear are multiplying forward
as we are trowelling down the furrows backwards.
The swedes are left to densely roll their thickness
around a core that hardens as it cleans.
We bend and bend, come up for air between
the rills and pushes. Where does this field end?

Yards from the far hedge we're bushed and bested.
Our rows have ended though the corner jeers.
From here it looks as though we've planned our answers.
When these are raked, layered in the mangel house,
we come to view just what was saved, torch a light
against this hardness, piled, fronding in the dark.

Canola

Far from the astronomers and the counsellors,
the princess gathers her most loyal courtiers
to the safe landing-place for underlings.

If we arrange ourselves like this, she says,
bending her supple back to reveal the lemon suns,
we will survive the collapse of everything we know.

Her maids try the pose, decide it's surprisingly comfortable.
"In the coming times there will be travellers
who'll look from their windows past the subtle greens

stunned by our parade of brightest yellow.
Rape they will say, knowingly, as the word turns
into something like oil on their tongue."

III
Cross-Talk

i. Shearling

We were warned against association, the danger of foot in mouth.
Five hours in the dark lurch of an unlicensed lorry. Smuggle:
the word becomes me, wool springs in its g g. Ink on our sides
shows we know our place between rights. But the grass is not sweeter,
no matter which side of the divide. Like Border Scots, our sisters,
we have no basis in *fact*. Yet with my jewel eye closed
I find my patch. Who makes a right? They don't tell us sheep.

ii. Majesty

Seven centuries later, respect for the sovereign was rife
among those who should know better but they coveted
the golden life, admired the way he dressed, like a cardinal
or bishop. They ground down the soft stone of the west
and the basalt of the northern tip and laid a trail
from there to here so he would be already home before he left.

Oh prince, how many parliaments can fit onto a small island?
How long can you conga a snake of deputies?
And as for *payoff, check-out, flip side, watch your back,*
it's a cultural condition with no known cure.

iii. Aisling

He's been wasting away for two years
since he saw a girl in his sleep.
She's in the shape of a bird every other month.

Which months is she in the shape of a girl?
She speaks to him from her severed head,
her voice from a gannet's beak:

We live in the land of the floating voter,
honour where honour does not bind.

How could presumption have ended
here where we've always presumed?

iv. Preparation

Rip the veil, say we were wrong,
call *de Valera* by his real name.
Pull down the blind of neutrality.
Sacrifice unnoticed cannot redeem.

How to get out of being ourselves
when we spent so long becoming?
Our doubt has lungs.
That's why we shout.
Are we ready to take a rompering?

v. Terror

Limbs that won't heal
Bedsores to be dressed
Kneecaps to keep steel caps
Excellence in prosthetics

It's easy enough to love a ghost, they say.
But what whisper would prepare their mothers?

vi. Fellow Traveller

We too have known the school of hard knocks,
have steered through narrow water.
We learned to swallow the queen's shilling
till it slid down our craw.

We plied the framed against the fake
until our state within a state
had owned us as colluders.

There is a crossing after all.
It's been approved.

We're on our way to sign
the long books of condolence.

Notes

p.13 'The ripening of an R.U.C. man': The Royal Ulster Constabulary (R.U.C.) was the police force in Northern Ireland from 1922-2001, when it was reconstituted as the Police Service of Northern Ireland (PSNI), as part of the peace process.

p.14 'Campbell': this name is thought to be the translation of Camhaoil, the Gaelic for crooked mouth or twisted lip.

p.24 'The Enthusiast' is a 'found poem'. It is taken from a toast of the 1690s used by the Orange society, The Aldermen of Skinner's Alley.

p.44 'Sinister':, Citóg is the Gaelic word for a left-handed person.

p.55 'Bedding': bonamh is a traditional word for piglet.

Acknowledgements

Thanks are due to the editors of the following where some of these poems or versions of them appeared: *Agenda Magazine, Brand, Cyphers, Crannóg, Magma, Mslexia, National Poetry Competition chapbook, nthposition, Oxford Magazine, Poetry*(Chicago), *Poetry Ireland Review, Rhythm, The Irish Times, The Southern Review, Something beginning with P: New Poems from Irish Poets, Wigtown Poetry Compilation, Wasafiri.*

Thanks are also due to the editors of the following where some of these poems were reprinted or recorded: *Oxfam Poetry CD, Lifelines 2*, compiled by Todd Swift; *Festschrift for Ciarán Carson, From the Small Back Room*, edited by W. R. Irvine, Netherlea Press, Belfast; *That Water Speaks in Tongues*, Templar Poetry, Derbyshire; Michael Marks Poetry Award pamphlet of shortlisted poets, 2009; *Poems of Protest* on ProtestPoems.org; *Snakeskin Poetry* Webzine.

A special thanks to those who read this work at an early stage, particularly Katie Donovan, Jean O'Brien and Seamus Cashman; to my colleagues at Kingston University London for their support and to members of the Stephen's Green workshop who suggested important revisions. The critical acumen of poet S.J. Litherland has been invaluable and was gratefully received. Appreciation is due to The Airfield Trust, Dublin, for a writer's residency which was jointly facilitated by the Arts Office of Dun Laoghaire/Rathdown County Council.

About the author:

Siobhán Campbell was born in Dublin. She spent a number of years in New York and San Francisco and worked as Director of Wolfhound Press before joining Faculty at Kingston University in London. Widely published in the USA and UK, she has won awards in the National, Troubadour, Mslexia and Wigtown International competitions. Her other collections are *The Permanent Wave* and *The cold that burns*, (Blackstaff Press) and chapbooks *That Water Speaks in Tongues* (Templar Poetry) – shortlisted for the Michael Marks Poetry Award – and *Darwin among the machines* (Rack Press). Her work is anthologized widely including in *Women's Work: Modern Women Poets writing in English* (Seren), *The Field Day Anthology of Irish Literature* (NYU Press) and *Identity Parade: New British and Irish Poets* (Bloodaxe). She has broadcast her work on BBC and RTE radio and given readings in Ireland, the UK and North America including at the Berkeley University reading series, Ottawa International Festival of Literature, Cúirt Festival in Galway and Poetry Now in Dublin.